YOUR KNOWLEDGE HAS VALUE

AF135733

UAV Inspection of Large Components. Adaptive Navigation at Runtime

Michelle Bettendorf

Bibliographic information published by the German National Library:

The German National Library lists this publication in the National Bibliography; detailed bibliographic data are available on the Internet at http://dnb.dnb.de.

ISBN: 9783346584663
This book is also available as an ebook.

Print and binding: Books on Demand GmbH, Norderstedt, Germany
Printed on acid-free paper from responsible sources.

The present work has been carefully prepared. Nevertheless, authors and publishers do not incur liability for the correctness of information, notes, links and advice as well as any printing errors.

GRIN web shop: https://www.grin.com/document/1162994

Abstract

In this thesis, two problems were covered. The first one is to estimate the position of a drone out of two different given transformations, which don't have the same coordinate origin. Furthermore, measurement errors have to be outbalanced so that the position estimation is as accurate as possible. In order to solve this problem, a Kalman Filter was utilised. The second problem is to direct the drone to given goal positions while avoiding obstacles. For directing the drone to the desired location a vector flight control with temporary goals was created. The vector flight control is working online and is constantly using the current estimated position of the Kalman Filter in order to direct the drone correctly at each time. This thesis is covering the concept, the implementation and evaluation of these algorithms.

Contents

CHAPTER 1

Problem definition

There are multiple projects, where drones are utilized for inspecting constructs. For example railway tracks, airbus planes or buildings are checked for errors and safety issues. These inspections are all carried out manually. This thesis is going to discuss the problem of automating the inspection of a large construct like a ship hull. Until now, humans inspect the hull by checking every screw and rivet if it is placed correctly. Performing the inspection automatically by a drone would be way easier, more time-efficient and more precise. One camera and the drone odometry are needed to inspect such a construct. The position of the drone needs to be determined by both sources. The drone's odometry specifies how far the drone is away from its starting point. From this data, the position of the robot relative to the starting point has to be computed and the camera determines the position of the robot relative to the construct. Measurement errors need to be filtered. It has to be determined at which position and with which orientation all the items like screws can be seen from the drone's camera. A list of positions combined with the orientations needs to be created. A trajectory over this list has to be computed. With the computed position of the drone, it has to be determined at which point of the trajectory the robot is and how to get to the new desired point of the trajectory. Control errors need to be considered. Furthermore, collisions have to be detected, in order to not collide with humans or other obstacles. In case of an unplanned object being in the way of the trajectory, an alternative trajectory needs to be computed in real-time.

In our approach, the position estimation from the camera of the construct is given from a 3rd party position estimation tool. The position estimation from the odometry of the robot is given from the drone, the DJI Mavic2, itself. Furthermore, the transformation between the camera and the odometry of the drone is known. In another thesis, the positions combined with the orientations for inspecting the objects are already computed and stored in a list. The DJI Mavic 2 drone will automatically stop in case of any collisions.

Since these problems are already solved, this thesis will focus on determining the position of the drone relative to the starting point by fusing the given data of the two position estimation tools, which will be referred to as the topic sensor fusion. The problems with fusing the data from the sensors are: how to detect errors in the sensor data, how to transfer all the data to the robotic framework of the Robot Operating System (ROS), how to get the actual drone position relative to the construct out of the data and what output should be created for the future work.

Furthermore, this thesis is going to cover the aspects of computing a trajectory over the list of the target positions combined with the orientations, determining at which point of the trajectory the drone is and how to get the robot to the new desired point. This will be referred to as the topic of trajectory planning. The problems with trajectory planning are: transferring the given data to ROS, finding the correct approach for planning the trajectory, creating a trajectory over all given location points, avoiding collisions with the construct and having a trajectory, which is actually feasible for the drone. Furthermore, there is the problem of letting the drone fly the planned trajectory. The difficulty is to receive the information at which point of the trajectory the robot currently is and how to direct the drone to fly the planned trajectory.

CHAPTER 2

Related work

In this chapter, other projects using drones for inspection will be discussed, then related sensor fusion work and in the end similar trajectory planning projects will be covered. The paper of McAree et al. [MAV16] covers the topic of a semi-autonomous drone, which has been developed for structural inspections. The fundamental idea is that the drone autonomously holds a safe distance to the structure so that the remote pilot can focus on the data collection from the camera. The used sensor for determining the distance to the structure is a laser sensor [MAV16]. Even though a fully autonomous drone is used for this thesis, some aspects of the paper can be used. For the autonomous part, the robotic framework Robot Operating System (ROS) was chosen, because of its advantages like its distributed nature [MAV16]. In that paper, the simulation of the drone is made with Gazebo and ROS because it is transferable to the real robot without much change in the code. For the simulation of the actual drone the simulator package AR.Drone 2.0 from the Technical University of Munich was used [MAV16]. The idea of using that simulation, ROS and Gazebo will be discussed in chapter 5 Implementation.

Another similar project is presented in the paper "Autonomous Flight Drone with Depth Camera for Inspection Task of Infra Structure" by S. Kawabata et al. [Kaw+18]. Their goal is to inspect infrastructures like buildings and bridges. They utilize companion computers mounted on to the drones which use MAVLink protocol for the autonomous flying [Kaw+18]. The drone utilized from S. Kawabata et al. is equipped with one depth camera. The infrastructure, which has to be inspected, doesn't have any cameras or sensors. For mapping, they chose the Simultaneous Localization and Mapping (SLAM) technique because in their case a 3D map is provided [Kaw+18].

For combining sensor data SLAM can be an option as well. The solution from T. Zhang et al. [Zha+14] utilizes SLAM on Monte Carlo Methods. The problem described in that paper is how to create a map of a room which has components such as glass, smooth wood or sponge material by a robot. The robot has two different sensors: a sonar sensor/ sonar ring and a 2D laser sensor. The solution is to use two intelligent layers of filters, the GlassDetect Layer, which can detect glass material and prevents errors from glass reflection and the CornerAdjust Layer, which adjusts corners to be as accurate as possible. Furthermore, a 2D SLAM algorithm is used [Zha+14]. As that project is using a 2D algorithm it can't be directly transferred to this thesis, because a 3D algorithm is needed. As also mentioned in the work of S. Kawabata et al. [Kaw+18] SLAM doesn't provide a 3D mapping for autonomous navigation for most of the cases. Furthermore, our setup is different, as the odometry of the drone is used instead of a sonar and a laser sensor.

Another option for combining sensor data is used in the paper "A trajectory tracking and 3D positioning controller for the AR.Drone quadrotor" by L. V. Santana et al. [San+14]. A simple Kalman Filter is used to track the position of the robot. Multiple sensors like a magnetometer and an ultrasonic sensor, provided by the AR.Drone, are used. They chose the simple Kalman Filter because of its less difficult implementation even though the extended Kalman Filter would work better [San+14]. As in our project we need to deal with non-linearity, because of the non-linear acceleration of the drone, a simple Kalman Filter without any linearization won't work. On the other hand, an extended Kalman Filter, which is especially designed for non-linear system dynamics, or a linearization before using the simple Kalman Filter can work. In the paper "Using the Kalman Filter in the Quadrotor Vehicle Trajectory Tracking System" by S. A. Belokon' et al. [Zol+13] it was tested how precise the estimation of the Extended Kalman Filter for an unmanned aerial vehicle is. The setup was an AR.Drone by Parrot, which consists of two video cameras, whereas only one of them was used in an indoor environment. The vehicle had to perform trajectories and the estimation error of the Extended Kalman Filter was measured. The average deviation was 0.2m [Zol+13]. This paper shows that even with one camera a pretty accurate estimation can be created by the Extended Kalman Filter. Therefore, the idea of using a Kalman Filter for the state estimation will be utilized in this thesis.

For trajectory planning a solution is proposed by Y. Bouktir et al. [BHC08]. Their aim is to create a simple numerical method to solve the inverse dynamical model of the drone. The conclusion of that paper is, that between the desired target points, a set of a minimum of five control points has to be created [BHC08]. The idea of having control points between the view points in order to get more accuracy about the robot's position and to have a simpler movement from one point to another will be transferred to our project.

Another similar project to ours is covered in the paper "Sampling-Based Coverage Path Planning for Inspection of Complex Structures" by B. Englot and F. S. Hover [EH12]. Their goal is to find a feasible path in an in-water ship hull for an autonomous inspection. The robot is equipped with one sensor. The conclusion of the paper is a sampling-based algorithm, which is a specific iteratively shortened roadmap algorithm [EH12]. In our approach, the ship hull is not underwater and an additional camera on the construct is set. The idea of an iterative solution to create some control points to reach between the given view points, will be utilized in this thesis.

CHAPTER 3

Basics

In this thesis, a large construct has to be inspected. For this Quadrocopters are utilized. In order to know the position of the robot, frames are used for the description of the location. For the representation of the rotation Quaternions are utilized. This information is processed by the Robot Operating System in order to control the Quadrocopter. Furthermore, the Robot Operating System supports the Unified Robot Description Format. With the help of this format, the drone's structure can be described. As the robot's location is not always known, an estimation is needed. For this, a Kalman Filter can be utilized. In order to navigate the drone to the goal, a feasible trajectory is needed. The Potential Field Method provides a solution for this.

3.1 Quadrocopter

A quadrocopter is an Unmanned Aerial Vehicle (UAV), which can be remotely controlled, partly or fully autonomously [Ben19]. It consists of four rotors, which are located on the same level and typically with an equal distance to the center point of the drone. In order to have a stable flight without any torque, the two opposite located rotors have the same turning direction, whereas the other pair rotates in the other direction. As a conclusion, there is one left turning and one right turning pair of rotors. A quadrotor, a short form of quadrocopter, has three directions of rotation, shown in figure 3.1. These are called roll-pitch-yaw. Roll is a motion around the x-axis, pitch is the same movement around the y-axis and yaw is the equivalent rotation of the z-axis [RG12].

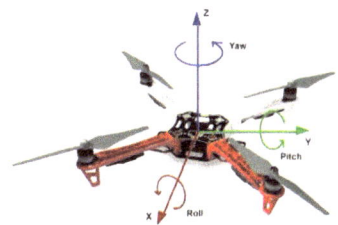

Figure 3.1: Roll Pitch Yaw of a Quadrocopter [RRA16]

In order to describe and to control the position of the drone frames are utilized.

3.2 Frames

With the intention of describing translations and rotations of the robot in space, a frame is determined. Every object such as the object, which has to be inspected, the drone, the world etc. has at least one frame [SNS16]. The object, which has to be inspected, will from now on be referred to as construct. Aiming to make a connection between the different frames, transformation matrices with the form 4 x 4 are created. These consist of a translation, which is defined as a 3 x 1 matrix [Sha+11] and a rotation, that is described as a 3 x 3 matrix [Cho92]. The following figure shows the general form of a matrix, which transforms the frame i to the coordinate system j.

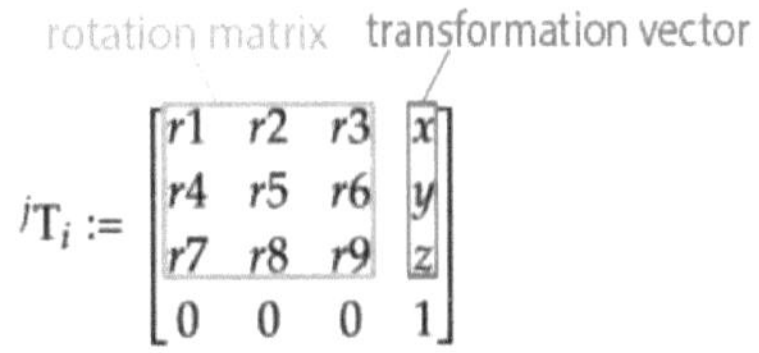

$$
{}^{j}T_i := \begin{bmatrix} r1 & r2 & r3 & x \\ r4 & r5 & r6 & y \\ r7 & r8 & r9 & z \\ 0 & 0 & 0 & 1 \end{bmatrix}
$$

rotation matrix   transformation vector

Figure 3.2: Transformation Matrix

The rotation angle can be computed from the rotation matrix with the help of the mathematical functions sine and cosine [Sla99]. There is one major problem with using matrices for transformation. For some rotation angles, there is no certain solution because of the periodic behaviour of the mathematical functions cosine and sine [Sla99]. Furthermore, there is the possibility of a gimbal lock, which causes a loss of a degree of freedom [HO18]. A possible solution are Quaternions.

3.3 Quaternions

Quaternions can be utilized to avoid problems like the gimbal lock. They are described with the help of complex numbers. By using quaternions the rotation of the coordinate system can be expressed. The general form of a quaternion is [Cho92]:

$$
\alpha = \alpha_0 + \alpha_1 i + \alpha_2 j + \alpha_3 k \tag{3.1}
$$

A quaternion consists of the real parameters α_0, α_1, α_2 and α_3 and of the orthogonal unit spatial vectors i, j and k [Cho92]. Whereas $i^2 = j^2 = k^2 = i * j * k = -1$ [Fin+62].

With the help of the quaternions, the rotation of the drone can be described. The computation of quaternions and frames is complex. With the aim to control the drone, a framework is needed. For this the Robot Operating System can be used.

3.4 Robot Operating System

With the intention of controlling and moving the robot, the robotic framework Robot Operating System (ROS) was created. ROS is an open source meta operating system for robots, which is language independent. The framework provides libraries and tools in order to help software developers create robot applications. ROS is built as a peer-to-peer network, where multiple communication methods like services (synchronized communication) and topics (asynchronous communication) are used [Fou13]. For visualizing information like the location of the frames, the graphical interface RVIZ can be utilized [Ste20]. The simulator Gazebo has been developed for simulating robots [Fou14]. With the interest of using a robot in ROS, it has to be parametrized. For this, the Unified Robot Description Format can be utilized.

3.5 Unified Robot Description Format

With the aim of controlling a robot, first the robot has to be described. In order to reach that goal the Unified Robot Description Format (URDF) can be utilized. It is an XML specification, which consists of link and joint elements of the robot. The joints are the connection between the links [Fou12]. With the help of URDF the robot can be described so that it can be controlled through ROS. The position of the drone can be described by using frames and quaternions. If the position is not determined or if errors may appear, a position estimation is needed. For this, the Kalman Filter can be used.

3.6 Kalman Filter

A Kalman Filter can estimate the system states quite accurately. It doesn't even have to have the precise nature of the system to make a precise estimation, which can be of the past, present or future. The Kalman Filter's concept is to fuse different sensors and to outbalance the upcoming measurement errors. In order to achieve that a model is created. This model has a predict step, which estimates the current position of the robot. With the update step measurements from the sensors can be integrated in real time. The model of the Kalman Filter utilizes a linear dependency between the system states $x \in \mathbb{R}^n$ [WB+95]:

$$x_{k+1} = \mathbf{A_k}x_k + \mathbf{B}u_k + w_k \tag{3.2}$$

A is an n x n matrix which connects the states of the time step k and step $k + 1$ to each other without regarding process noise. The input $u \in \mathbb{R}$ is related to the state x by the n x l matrix **B** [WB+95]. In order to have process noise represented the variable w_k is created randomly [WVDM00]. The measurements $z \in \mathbb{R}^m$ are represented in the equation [WB+95]:

$$z_k = \mathbf{H_k}x_k + v_k \tag{3.3}$$

H is an m x n matrix, which connects the measurement z_k to the state x_k [WB+95], whereas v_k is the representation of the observation noise [WVDM00].

3.6.1 Extended Kalman Filter

The Kalman Filter is only working for a linear process and for linear measurements. With the aim of having a non-linear process and/or non-linear measurements the extended Kalman Filter (EKF) was invented. The equations (3.2) and (3.3) are changed to:

$$x_{k+1} = f(x_k, u_k, w_k) \tag{3.4}$$

$$z_k = h(x_k, v_k) \tag{3.5}$$

The tasks of the matrices **A** and **B** are executed by a non-linear function f. Accordingly the non-linear function h replaces the matrix **H**. It is assumed, that f and h are known [WB+95].

3.6.2 Unscented Kalman Filter

The Extended Kalman Filter uses linearization in order to calculate the uncertainty. Due to the linearization, the approximation can contain errors. With the aim of minimising the approximation error, the Unscented Kalman Filter (UKF) was created. The UKF utilizes a minimal set of the measurements, in order to be more error-prone. The random variables w_k and v_k are calculated using the method of the unscented transformation with the goal of getting representative nonlinear transformations [WVDM00]. In conclusion, the Kalman Filter is working for estimating the system state in a linear context, the Extended Kalman Filter is the equivalent for a non-linear context and the Unscented Kalman Filter is optimizing the Extended Kalman Filter in order to have even more precise approximations of the system state [WVDM00] [WB+95].

The Kalman Filter is used to estimate the position of the drone. This is needed for planning a trajectory.

3.7 Trajectory planning

For understanding the trajectory planning process first, the word path needs to be defined. A path is a sequence of points from a starting point to a target point. It is only a geometrical description of the movement. A trajectory is a path added with the dimension of the time [BM08]. By the Lexico dictionary [Lex20] a trajectory is defined as "[t]he path followed by a projectile flying or an object moving under the action of given forces." A trajectory between two given points is called a point-to-point (PTP) trajectory. There is the option of having a trajectory between multiple points, which is called a multipoint trajectory. Furthermore, there is the distinction between one-dimensional and multi-dimensional trajectories [BM08]. For planning such a trajectory two different concepts exist: online and offline planning. The concept of offline planning is to compute the entire trajectory from the starting to the target position before the beginning of the movement. Whereas the online planning concept is to compute the trajectory during the movement in order to react to collisions, errors during the motion or a change in the target position [Shi15]. An example of online planning is the potential field method.

3.8 Potential Field

An approach for path planning is the potential field method. Based on the configuration of the robot, artificial potential forces are computed. These forces determine the movement of the robot [Pet15]. Every point in the world is assigned to an artificial potential field, which is either an attractive or a repulsive field. The robot's goal is to move to the lowest potential, the target position. The obstacles, which should be avoided by the robot, are marked as high potentials [Sid18]. In order to create a path, two planners are needed: a global and a local planner. The global one selects a path out of the lowest potentials and the local planner modifies the path so that every possible dynamic collision is avoided [HA+92]. For generating a force of attraction for a 2D system the following function is used [Sid18]:

$$P_g = C\sqrt{|x - x_{goal}|^2 + |y - y_{goal}^2|} \tag{3.6}$$

The coordinates of the starting position are named x and y and the coordinates of the goal position are called x_{goal} and y_{goal}, whereas the constant C is predefined. On the other hand are repulsive forces [Sid18]. For these, a maximum distance has to be determined, so that there isn't an infinite increasing force [Pet15]. Furthermore, it is the distribution of repulsive forces by the boundaries and repulsive forces by the obstacles. An utilized function for repulsive forces by the boundaries for 2D is [Sid18]:

$$P_{HA} = \frac{1}{\delta + \sum_{i=1}^{s}(g_i + |g_i|)} \tag{3.7}$$

Whereas the linear function g_i reflects the border of the surroundings. The symbol s represents the amount of boundary segments and δ is a predefined constant number, which is normally assigned a small value. The repulsive forces by the obstacles for 2D can be calculated with the following formula [Sid18]:

$$p_{i,j} = \frac{p_{max}}{1 + g} \tag{3.8}$$

where

$$g(x,y) = (x_0 - \frac{l}{2} - x) + |x_0 - \frac{l}{2} - x| + (x - x_0 - \frac{l}{2} + 1) + |x - x_0 - \frac{l}{2} + 1| \tag{3.9}$$
$$+ (y_0 - \frac{l}{2} - y) + |y_0 - \frac{l}{2} - y| + (y - y_0 - \frac{l}{2} + 1) + |y - y_0 - \frac{l}{2} + 1|$$

In equation 3.8 the highest potential is called p_{max}, whereas in equation 3.9 the obstacle is described by the coordinates of the center x_0 and y_0 and the side length l. An example of a resulting potential field out of the attracting and repulsive forces is shown in figure 3.3 [Sid18]:

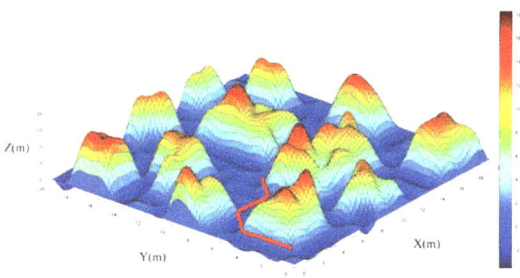

Figure 3.3: Potential Field in 3D [Sid18]

This graphic shows the obstacle detection. Through the potential field method maxima are created, where the obstacles are and minima, where the collision-free cells are.
One problem that occurs is the local minima trap. This arises if the attracting force of the goal and the repulsive forces cancel each other out. In conclusion, the robot stays in the local minimum and won't reach the goal [Sid18]. An example of a local minima trap is shown in figure 3.4.

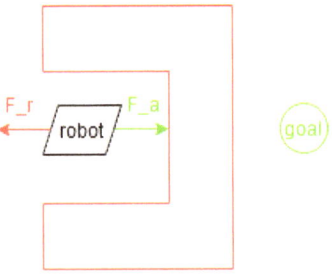

Figure 3.4: Local Minima Trap

This figure shows a robot, a boundary and a goal. The goal is colored green and the boundary is colored red. F_r stands for repulsive force and F_a resembles the attractive force, which are induced through the boundary and the goal. Because of the potential field method, the robot ended up in the shown position. The problem with that location is that the overall force is zero. Due to that, the robot is not moving anymore, even though the goal is not reached and there could be a possibility to reach it.
In order to solve the local minima trap two approaches are utilized. The first one is to modify the potential field functions in order to erase every local minimum. The robot would never end up in a situation as shown in figure 3.4. The second approach is to develop a method so that the robot is able to escape from local minima. One method for solving this problem is the random walk, which consists of letting the robot move in a random direction for a random amount of time and then starting the potential field method again. Another possibility is to change to a wall-following algorithm for a certain amount of time and then switching back to the potential field method [XK97]. These two methods are not the only ones existing for escaping local minima. The other solutions won't be discussed in this thesis, because they won't be utilized and the explanation would go beyond the scope of this work.

CHAPTER 4

Concept

The general concept of this thesis is structured in two parts, the sensor fusion and the trajectory planning. The goal is to compute a stabilised transformation out of the data from the odometry of the drone, which computes the position of the drone relative to its starting point and from a software tool, which determines the location of the robot relative to the origin of the construct. The data from the odometry of the drone can deviate over time from the actual position. Furthermore, it is possible that the software tool has some jumps. The sensor fusion is needed in order to have a precise position estimation, which offsets these errors. In figure 4.1 the connections of the frames and the transformations are illustrated. The frame of the construct origin and of the drone are given. Furthermore, the transformation between the starting point and the drone and between the construct origin and the drone can be computed. In this approach, it is assumed, that the starting point of the drone is within the field of view of the construct camera. Therefore, the starting point is known from the start of the drone and the transformation between the starting point and the construct origin can be calculated. With the help of the Kalman Filter and the transformations a new frame, the stabilised transformation, can be created.

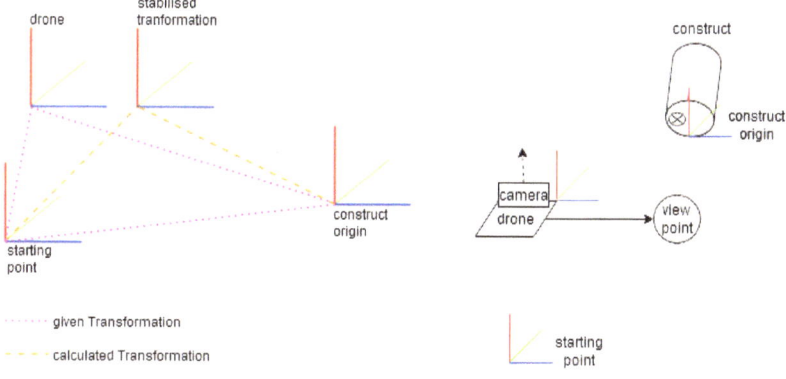

Figure 4.1: Frames Diagram   Figure 4.2: View Point Diagram

Out of the transformation from the starting point to the stabilised transformation and of a sequence of view points a vector flight control will be planned in the second part of this thesis. View points are the already calculated positions with orientations, from where the drone can inspect all the necessary parts of the construct. This is shown in figure 4.2. In this figure, the frames for construct origin, starting point and drone are shown. The construct origin is placed in the construct and has one component, which should be inspected by the drone. This component is illustrated as a cross. The drone frame is placed in the drone. Furthermore, the drone has a camera integrated. The camera has a viewing direction, which is shown with a dotted arrow. The view point is already computed. It has the position and orientation from which the drone can inspect the components of the construct. The goals are to direct the drone to every view point while avoiding static obstacles, which are given by a CAD File, to have the shortest possible way to the view points and to have feasible movements. With the help of the potential field method, a vector flight control with these requirements can be calculated. The vector flight control is an online trajectory planning method, which calculates vectors to direct the drone towards the view point. The potential field method has one disadvantage, local minima traps can occur. For solving local minima traps the concept of the random walk will be utilized, which will be explained in 4.2.

The detailed concept will be explained in 4.1 and 4.2. In 4.3 an overview of the architecture will be given.

4.1 Sensor Fusion of drone odometry and inspection software

In this thesis, the position of the drone needs to be estimated out of the information given from the drone and from a software tool. For fusing the data from the position estimation of the drone and from the software tool it has to be considered, that the coordinate systems have different origins. The drone estimates its position relative to the starting point. The software tool on the other hand estimates the location of the robot relative to the construct. A calculation between these different coordinate frames is needed. After finishing this calculation the sensor data will be fusioned by a Kalman Filter. Due to the fact that the system is non-linear because of the non-linear acceleration of the drone, it has to be linearized. For the linearization, the mean velocity for each axis direction (x, y, z) for every actualisation step will be calculated. The used equation for x, where x is the current x position, x_{prior} is the latest x position and Δt is the time difference between the current and the latest x position, is:

$$v_x = \frac{x - x_{prior}}{\Delta t} \tag{4.1}$$

Accordingly, the linearization of y and z takes place. Afterwards, the Kalman Filter can be used. The estimated position from the Kalman Filter will be used for the trajectory planning. The concept of the trajectory planning will be discussed in the next chapter.

4.2 Vector Flight Control

In this project, a feasible path, which is as short as possible and collision-free has to be computed out of a sequence of given view points. The planning will be done online due to the fact, that the stabilised position from the Kalman Filter will be generated during runtime. The concept is to have a vector flight control,which directs the drone through the computed artificial potential field by using vectors. With a view to the realization of this concept, temporary goals need to be defined. These won't be reached and are intended for determining the flying direction of the drone. In order to have this project extendable, no information about the maximum distance between the view points can be considered. The result is that a fixed amount of temporary goals can't be chosen beforehand. The amount has to be chosen during runtime. An approach for solving this problem is using an iterative method so that one temporary goal is computed at a time. After a certain amount of time and before reaching the temporary goal, another one has to be computed and given as a new direction. This will be repeated until the temporary goal is equal or within a certain deviation to the view point, in order to fly the robot directly to it. Furthermore, it has to be determined at which deviation the view point is considered as reached. The concept of the temporary goals is shown in figure 4.3.

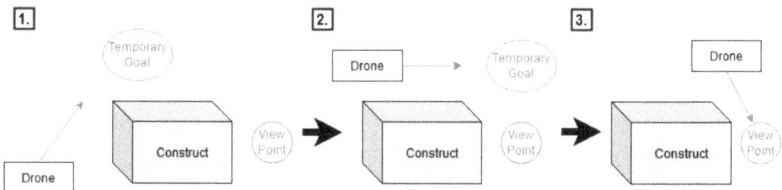

Figure 4.3: Potential Field Method

In this figure, the drone, a view point and the construct are illustrated. The drone has to fly around the construct to get to the view point. In order to accomplish this, a temporary goal is computed through the potential field method in step one. In the second step, the new position of the drone is given by the Kalman Filter. The temporary goal from step one is not reached, yet but a new temporary goal further towards the view point is calculated and set as the new direction for the drone. The same procedure happens in step three, except that the new temporary goal has only a small deviation to the view point, so that the view point can be seen as the new goal. The difference to the temporary goals is that it is aimed to reach the view point. A view point is reached if the drone is within a certain distance to it. This algorithm is repeated until every view point is reached. After this procedure, all the given components of the construct are inspected. The problem with the potential field method is that local minima traps, shown in figure 3.4, can appear. For solving this problem the random walk method will be utilized. The random walk method is illustrated in figure 4.4. In this figure, the local minima trap is shown in the first step. The potential field method doesn't provide any vectors for escaping this trap and reaching the goal. For solving this problem, the potential field method will be switched off for the second step. In this step, the random walk method is applied. The robot is moving in a random direction, which doesn't collide with the obstacle, for a random amount of time. This is illustrated with the black arrow. Afterwards, the robot is in the position of step three. Here the potential field method takes place again. The attractive force, called F_a, and the repulsive force, called F_r, are computed. With the help of these, the result force (F_res) can be computed. Through the result force, a new temporary goal can be calculated. Accordingly to figure 4.3 are the steps four to six. New temporary goals are computed during runtime and the robot is navigated until the goal is reached. In figure 4.4 the local minima trap is solved by using the random walk method once. It can occur that this method is not solving the problem within one step. For this, the method has to be repeated multiple times until a way out of the trap is found. Furthermore, there is the possibility that there is no way out of the local minima trap. This can be checked if the random walk method doesn't find a solution within a certain amount of time. If this is the case, the robot will return to its starting position and land.

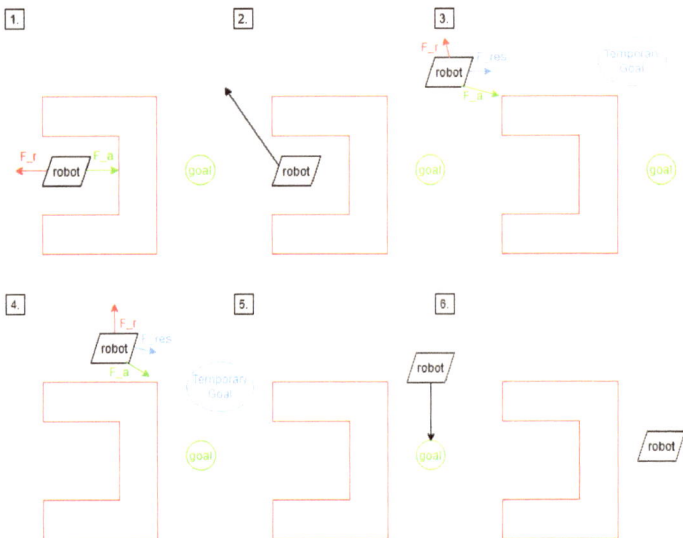

Figure 4.4: Escaping the local minima

With the interest of getting a full overview of the architecture of the sensor fusion combined with the vector flight control, the following chapter is summarising the chapters 4.1 and 4.2.

4.3 Architecture Overview

This chapter is summarising the chapters 4.1 and 4.2 in order to give an overview of the whole concept of this thesis. For illustration purposes, the figure 4.5 was created. In this figure the sensor fusion concept is colored orange, the vector flight control concept is colored green and already existing parts of the project are colored in grey. In the beginning of this thesis the odometry of the drone provides the position of the drone relative to the starting point and the position relative to the construct is given by the simulation. Because they have different coordinate systems a computation of the difference between them has to be created. Therefore, a linearization of the data has to be computed. Afterwards, the data from the two input sources can be fusioned with the help of a Kalman Filter. The Kalman Filter gives an output, which contains a stabilised position. With that, the sensor fusion is finished. The stabilised position is needed for the vector flight control. The potential field method needs a stabilised position and a sequence of view points. The sequence of view points is already created in another thesis and can be used for this thesis. For simplification the creation of temporary goals is not listed separately, it is part of the potential field method. The outcome of the algorithm of the potential field is a new target position, which is a temporary goal or a view point, for the drone. After executing flying towards the new target position, the trajectory planning is finished. For being able to fly to more than one view point or temporary goal, the odometry of the drone needs to be updated. With the measurements of the drone's position after flying to a new target position, the odometry can be updated. This concept is the base of the implementation, which will be covered in chapter 5.

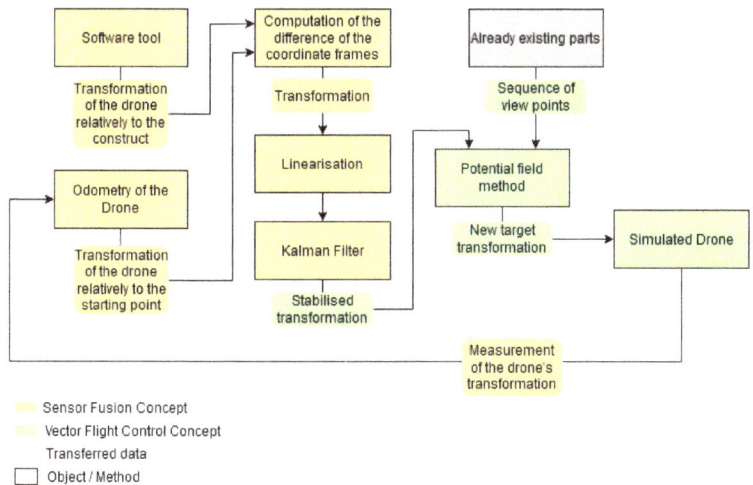

Figure 4.5: Concept Diagram

CHAPTER 5

Implementation

To implement a solution to the given problems of fusing the sensor data and creating a vector flight control two different ideas are needed. First, the sensor data topic will be covered, followed by the vector flight control. In both parts already existing implementation ideas of similar projects will be introduced and discussed whether it can be used for this thesis or not. Afterwards in each section, a solution of the implementation will be presented. The architecture provides the option of creating an online collision detection, but this won't be implemented in this thesis.

In this project, the robotic framework Robot Operating System (ROS) will be used, because the given drone can be controlled with this framework and it is already used in the other parts of the project. As the software tool providing the position of the drone relative to the construct is not yet available, a simulation has to be designed. The creation of the simulation will be covered in 5.1.2.

5.1 Kalman Filter Implementation

This section will cover the topic of the sensor fusion implementation. Section 5.1.1 covers the ideas of already existing solutions, section 5.1.2 describes the creation of a simulation of the inspection software and section 5.1.3 deals with the realization of a solution to the sensor fusion topic.

5.1.1 Existing libraries

One of the already existing ROS packages is the robot_pose_ekf package. The package gives a filtered output pose by using an extended Kalman filter. The filter has a 3D position and a 3D orientation model. It is designed for a wheeled robot due to the fact that the wheel odometry is measured [Mee12]. Because a drone is used for this thesis, this ROS package won't be utilized.

For ground-based and flying robots a package called robot_localisation package [Moo18] is available. It fuses input sensors and provides position estimations for any number of data sources. Furthermore, there is the choice of using the extended or the unscented Kalman Filter. On top of that, there is the possibility to not use all the given data from the sensors. With this package, the absence of continuous data is not a problem, because there is a continuous estimation of the position of the robot [met19]. The problem of these packages is that the Kalman Filter is already completely implemented and the parameters can't be changed to fit the needs of this thesis. Furthermore, this package is specified on particular sensors [Rat+15].

Less specified are the Bayes ++ Open Source Bayesian Filtering Classes. These are multiple C++ classes with a various number of numerical algorithms. Bayesian Filtering uses the technique of combining observations and a mathematical formula to estimate the position of the robot [Ste05]. The Bayes ++ Open Source Bayesian Filtering Classes don't have a trivial configuration. Furthermore, it is error-prone due to the fact that multiple objects have to be initiated by the user. For example a suitable C++ class has to be selected or the sampling and filtering has to be initiated periodically [Rat+15]. On the basis of this, the Bayes ++ Open Sources Bayesian Filtering Classes won't be utilized. The Generic Sensor Fusion Package for ROS is available to combine all possible sensors and is less error-prone than the Bayes ++ Open Source Bayesian Filtering Classes [Rat+15]. Implemented algorithms are the Kalman Filter, the Extended Kalman Filter, The Unscented Kalman Filter and Particle Filtering. The Generic Sensor Fusion Package consists of three parts, the C++ library, a generic ROS node and the configuration [Rat15]. This library was last updated in 2015 and is therefore not compatible with the used ROS distribution.

A different approach is using python libraries. The filterpy library provides a Kalman Filter class. It assumes the task of the calculations and offers a function for updating the states of the system. The user has to determine all the calculation matrices like the transition matrix [Lab20]. Based on the individual choice of the calculation matrices this library provides a kalman filter, which fits to the specific problem of the user. Because of this and that this library is compatible with the simulation of the software tool, section 5.1.2, it will be used for the realization. The realization will be explained in 5.1.3.

5.1.2 Simulation

The whole thesis will be realized in a simulation. In further work, it can be transferred to the hardware system. For a simulation environment RotorS will be utilized. The reason will be given in the section 5.2.1. With the help of the tf TransformListener, the position of the drone relative to its starting point and relative to the construct can be looked up. This simulates the data given by the drone and by the software tool. On top of that, the transformation from the construct to the starting point can be looked up. With this information, the data given from the TransformListener can be transformed in order to be relative to the starting point so that it can be used next to the data given from the drone. The realization of this simulation will be explained in the next chapter.

5.1.3 Realization

For the realization multiple nodes are needed, these are shown in figure 5.1. The class for the simulation tool is colored in purple, the one for the vector flight control is colored in green and the classes for the sensor fusion in orange. In this section first, the simulation tool will be explained and then the sensor fusion part will be covered. The vector flight control part will be covered in section 5.2.2. In figure 5.1 the nodes are ellipsis and the ROS package tf, which is used for keeping track of the multiple frames is a cuboid. The used RotorS simulation provides multiple nodes and topics for controlling the drone. As the detailed implementation of RotorS is not relevant for this thesis, it will be handled as a blackbox, which is shown in figure 5.1 as a circle. Every node is implemented in a different python class. The potential_field node is implemented in the move python class, the other nodes are implemented in the python classes with the same name as the node.

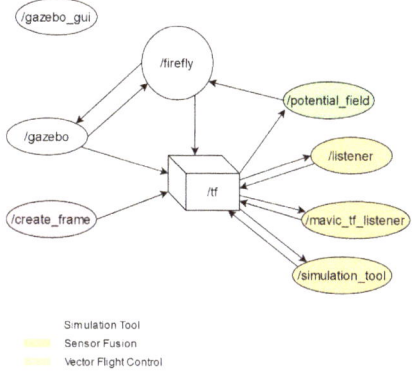

Figure 5.1: Rosgraph

In order to calculate transformations, the position of the construct, which is aimed to be inspected, has to be known. Furthermore, the construct origin is for the inspection software needed. As this has to be simulated in this thesis, the frame of the construct origin is created in the create_frame python class. It sends the position and orientation of the coordinate system to the ROS package tf through the sendTransform method provided by the TransformBroadcaster. The new frame is called object and has the translation (position array) and the rotation (orientation array) with regard to the world frame. The position and orientation array is hard-coded. The code is shown in the following listing. The new frame needs to be constantly sent to tf, that is the reason why there is a while loop.

```python
def create_coordinate_frame(position,orientation):
    br = tf.TransformBroadcaster()
    rate = rospy.Rate(10.0)
    while not rospy.is_shutdown():
        br.sendTransform((position[0], position[1], position[2]), (orientation[0],
            orientation[1], orientation[2], orientation[3]), rospy.Time.now(),
            "object","world")
        rate.sleep()

if __name__=='__main__':
    rospy.init_node('create_frame') #Initialising the node
    position = [2, 2, 2]
    orientation = [-0.002, -0.727, 0.242, 0.643]
    create_coordinate_frame(position,orientation)
```

Listing 5.1: Code from create_frame.py

In reality, the inspection software provides the position of the drone relative to the construct. In order to simulate this, the simulation_tool node looks up the transformation between the drone and the construct origin and publishes the received data to tf as a new coordinate system with the name 'correctedobject'. Equivalent is the function of the mavic_tf_listener node, which represents the drone odometry. It looks up the transformation between the drone and the starting point, called world, and publishes the data to tf as a new coordinate system with the name 'correctedmavic'. These two additional coordinate systems are furthermore needed to simulate the errors, which can appear in the real system. In the real system, the transformation between the drone and the starting point can deviate over time. In order to simulate this first, the transformation between the starting point and drone needs to be determined. Then over time, a variable needs to be incremented in order to have a constant increasing deviation. To realize this the variable i is incremented in each step. As using i directly for adding a deviation would be too much because each step would have an increasing deviation of 1m, the variable d (short for deviation) comes to place. It factorises i in order to have almost no deviation in the beginning and that it is slowly increasing. The deviation is added to the translation, which is received from the lookupTransform method and afterwards published to the new frame 'correctedmavic'. The code is shown in the following.

```
(trans,rot) = listener.lookupTransform('world', 'firefly/base_link',
    rospy.Time(0))
i += 1
d = i * 0.00001 #deviation
trans[0] = trans[0] + d
trans[1] = trans[1] + d
trans[2] = trans[2] + d
br.sendTransform(trans, rot, rospy.Time.now(), 'correctedmavic', 'world')
```

Listing 5.2: Code error drift

Equivalent is the realization of the simulation_tool class except that there is no constant deviation. The error in the simulation_tool is that due to bad camera tracking some jumps can happen. The implementation is similar to the mavic_tf_listener, there is a variable, called i, which is incremented over time. If this variable reaches certain numbers, a random deviation between one and four meters is added to the translation. In the simulation tool not only jumps are possible errors. The drone can be misplaced for a certain amount of time. For realizing this, a variable is created which is at the beginning set to the value -1 and after a certain amount of time changed to 1. This variable is multiplied to the translation. The result is that after a certain amount of time, this variable won't affect the translation, but in the beginning, the drone is misplaced. The new frame, created in this class, is called 'correctedobject'.
The code of the simulation_tool won't be shown, as it is similar to the last one shown. The created frames 'correctedmavic' and 'correctedobject' are needed for the listener class. The purpose of this class is to use a kalman filter to estimate the position of the drone. In order to use a kalman filter first, the transformation between the starting point and the 'correctedobject' frame and between the starting point and the 'correctedmavic' frame need to be looked up. From the lookup, the translation and rotation are given

---

between the coordinate frames. The rotation is provided in the form of a quaternion. To get the rotation angle, the w value from the quaternion is needed. For the calculation of the rotation angle, the arcus cosine will be used. This mathematical function is only defined from -1 until 1, whereas w can because of approximation errors reach a value slightly over 1 or slightly under -1. Therefore the maximum of w has to be set as 1 and the minimum as -1. The formula for the calculation of the angle is:

$$\alpha = acos(w) * 2 \tag{5.1}$$

For calculating the linearization the time difference is needed. For this, the current time needs to be saved. The pseudocode for this algorithm is shown in figure 5.2. As the lookup can't be done parallel first, the lookup between the starting point and the 'correctedobject' frame is done. For the linearization the time difference of the different states is needed. In order to get the respective time difference, the current time has to be saved directly after the lookup. Afterwards the value w is adapted as described. Before repeating this procedure for the 'correctedobject' frame, the values are used in the priorstate method, which will be explained in the following. In the interest of implementing the Kalman Filter, the library filterpy.kalman will be utilized. For this library two methods need to be implemented, the priorstate and the kalman function. First, the kalman method will be explained. This method has the function to determine the important matrices, which are F, H, B, R, Q and X, for the Kalman Filter. In chapter 3 some different denominations are used. F is the same as A, which connects the states from the time step k and step k+1 to each other without regarding process noise. Q is the same as w and represents the process noise and R is equivalent to v, which resembles the observation noise. The denomination for B, the input matrix, H, the matrix, which connects the measurement to the state, and X, the state matrix, is the same. The code for the kalman function is the following:

```
def kalman(x,y,z, vx, vy, vz, alpha, valpha, dt, timestamp, r=0.1, q=0.2):
    global kf
    kf = KalmanFilter(dim_x=8,dim_z=8)
    kf.F = np.array([[1.,dt,0.,0.,0.,0.,0.,0.],
            [0.,1.,0.,0.,0.,0.,0.,0.],
            [0.,0.,1.,dt,0.,0.,0.,0.],
            [0.,0.,0.,1.,0.,0.,0.,0.],
            [0.,0.,0.,0.,1.,dt,0.,0.],
            [0.,0.,0.,0.,0.,1.,0.,0.],
            [0.,0.,0.,0.,0.,0.,1.,dt],
            [0.,0.,0.,0.,0.,0.,0.,1.]])

    kf.H = np.array([[1.,0.,0.,0.,0.,0.,0.,0.],
            [0.,1.,0.,0.,0.,0.,0.,0.],
            [0.,0.,1.,0.,0.,0.,0.,0.],
            [0.,0.,0.,1.,0.,0.,0.,0.],
            [0.,0.,0.,0.,1.,0.,0.,0.],
            [0.,0.,0.,0.,0.,1.,0.,0.],
            [0.,0.,0.,0.,0.,0.,1.,0.],
            [0.,0.,0.,0.,0.,0.,0.,1.]])
```

```
kf.B = np.array([[0.,0.,0.,0.]]).T
kf.R *= r
kf.Q *= q
kf.x = np.array([[x,vx,y,vy,z,vz, alpha, valpha]]).T
xprior = x
yprior = y
zprior = z
alphaprior = alpha
return kf
```

Listing 5.3: Code Kalman Filter

First, it has to be declared how many states the Kalman Filter should predict. As we have the direction of the three-dimensional space, x, y, z, the rotation angle alpha and the corresponding velocities, 8 states need to be predicted. The state matrix is structured as [x, vx, y, vx, z, vz, alpha, valpha]^T, where v stands for velocity. The velocities are the derivation of the positions, that is the reason why the F matrix contains the symbol dt, which stands for derivation. Out of the first line of the state matrix, the x position is directly given, that is the reason why there is the one. Out of the x position the x velocity can be determined by using derivation, because of that dt stands in the second column of the first line. The other variables can't be determined out of the x position, that is why the rest of the line contains zeros. The second line of the state matrix contains the x velocity. Out of the x velocity, only the x velocity can be determined. In conclusion, only a single one is written in the second column of the second line. Equivalently are the other lines determined. The lines which are connected to the positions or the angle have additional to a single one also a deviation. The lines which are connected to the velocities only have a single one, because out of the velocity nothing else can be determined. The H matrix is similar to the F matrix, except that the velocities are already calculated in the priorstate function so that no deviation is needed. This matrix has only ones at the diagonal. The B matrix is filled with zeros because there is no input, which can change our system. The measurement and observation noise have the same factor in every element because the noises affect all the system states equally. The factor 0.2 for R and 0.2 for Q were determined by testing, which factors have the best outcome for this system. As this function is performed before the first priorstate function, the first prior states have to be determined, because they are needed for calculating the velocities. These are set to the initial given x, y, z, and alpha parameters. In the priorstate function the linearization takes place. For this, the equation 4.1 will be used for x, y, z and alpha. Out of these computations, the velocities in each direction and rotation are given. With these and the state variables x, y, z and alpha, the new measurement matrix Z (from equation 3.3) can be created. With the help of this matrix, the Kalman Filter can be updated. Due to the fact that not all errors can be outbalanced by the Kalman Filter, an additional filter has to be created. The purpose of the filter is to prevent jumps to influence the Kalman Filter. Jumps can happen from the simulation tool and should not affect the position estimation. To prevent this error an if statement is needed. For the if condition the distance from the current position of the drone to the prior position of the drone is calculated. If the value is more than 2, a jump happened. If there is no jump, the position of the drone couldn't change that fast. If a jump is detected, it is known that the current position doesn't resemble the actual position of the drone. As the jumps are only for a short amount of time, the current position is set as the same value as the prior position. The reason of that is to avoid having a completely wrong value and not having a value. The new current position is most likely not completely correct but is closer to the real position than the jump. In our approach, the values from the two sources are used one after the other. If a jump happens, the last given value is utilized, which is from the other source. As jumps don't happen in the data given from the 'correctedmavic' frame, the data is more accurate than only relying on the estimated position of the Kalman Filter. With this approach, jumps are not affecting the position estimation. In order to have the prediction of the position of the drone as accurate as possible, the predict method of the Kalman Filter will be performed after updating the Kalman Filter. To use the position predicted from the Kalman Filter, it has to be published as a coordinate frame to tf. The published coordinate frame is called kalman and will be updated every time the priorstate method is executed. The pseudocode for the priorstate method is shown in figure 5.3:

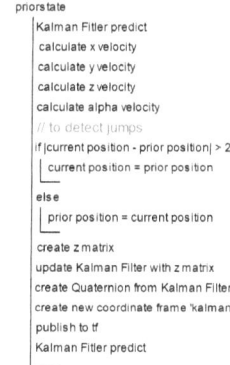

repeat while rospy is not shutdown

    lookup Transformation between starting point and 'correctedobject' frame

    get current time

    calculate time difference

    if w > 1

        w = 1

    if w < -1

        w = -1

    priorstate

    repeat for 'correctedobject' frame

    wait 2 seconds

priorstate

  Kalman Fitler predict

  calculate x velocity

  calculate y velocity

  calculate z velocity

  calculate alpha velocity

  // to detect jumps

  if |current position - prior position| > 2

    current position = prior position

  else

    prior position = current position

  create z matrix

  update Kalman Filter with z matrix

  create Quaternion from Kalman Filter

  create new coordinate frame 'kalman'

  publish to tf

  Kalman Fitler predict

Figure 5.2: Pseudocode loop in listener

Figure 5.3: Pseudocode priorstate function

This method is performed after looking up the transformation between starting point and the 'correctedobject' frame and between the starting point and the 'correctedobject' frame. The lookup is done every two seconds in order to be as accurate to the reality as possible. The calculated position from the Kalman Filter is needed in the potential field method in order to plan the new vector for each timestamp. The implementation of the potential field method will be covered in the following section.

5.2 Potential Field Method Implementation

In this section, the potential field method implementation will be discussed. The section 5.2.1 will present already existing libraries. Subsequently in 5.2.2 the realization of the potential field method is explained.

5.2.1 Existing libraries

For planning a trajectory the framework MoveIt was developed. It is a package originally designed for planning a trajectory for robot arms. MoveIt is planning the trajectory from the actual robot location to the given desired location by using inverse kinematics while checking for collisions [Con18a]. For collision checking the Fast Collision Library, which makes distance-checking capabilities available, is utilized. The planned trajectories are smooth due to path smothers and generators so that the robot can execute the movement. There is the possibility to react dynamically to the environment so that human interaction near the robot is safe [CSC12]. With Gazebo a simulation of the movement of the trajectory can be executed in a simulated environment. For planning a trajectory over multiple points there is also an option in MoveIt, which is called the move group. The move group is an interface, which can be used either in C++ or in python [Con18b]. MoveIt can be used to move the real robot [Con18a]. Quadrocopters can't use all of the features of MoveIt, which are necessary for this thesis. One example of a feature is the FollowJointTrajectory action, which is utilized to follow a trajectory by the robot. This is only possible for robot arms and not for drones. One aim of this thesis is to reach different points, for which in MoveIt the FollowJointTrajectory action would be needed. As this action can't be used, MoveIt can't be utilized.

Specifically for drones designed is the TeleKyb framework. The usage is the planning of the trajectory of the drone or a swarm of drones with human inputs. Through a trajectory processor obstacle avoidance can be implemented and through the trajectory behavior, the next desired position and velocity can be computed. Signal filtering libraries are used for computing the linear and angular velocities. The SwarmSimX Simulation is supported for the simulation [Gra+13]. This package is specifically designed for Quadrotors from MikroCopter and only for Ubuntu 12.04 LTS in combination with ROS Fuerte [AFG13]. This system is eight years old and isn't further developed. As for this project, another Quadrotor and a different ROS distribution is used, it isn't possible to utilize the TeleKyb framework.

In the master thesis "Optimal Trajectory Planning for a Quadrotor UAV for Autonomous DroneRace" [Nek19] multiple trajectory planning methods are analysed. The trajectories are planned using the FALCON.m toolbox for Matlab. For the implementation of the controller, the RotorS framework is utilized. The quadcopter controller node is subscribing to the odometry and waypoint messages. The controller is also publishing motor inputs. The conclusion is that nonlinear trajectories give the best results. The outcome of the polynomial ones is still in the acceptable range [Nek19]. The source code of this project is not available, but the idea of using the RotorS framework as a simulation for this thesis will be used. This framework contains multiple drone models and can be extended for the Kalman Filter and the Potential Field Method.

5.2.2 Realization

For this thesis, the simulation RotorS is utilized. As RotorS offers multiple drone models, one has to be chosen. In this thesis, the firefly drone will be used, as it has the best implementation to fit the needs of this thesis. In order to match the requirements of this thesis, some changes in RotorS need to be done. By running RotorS it can be seen, that the drone is pivoting a lot while flying to different points. Through pivoting the drone is more likely to collide with obstacles or to lose the balance and to crash. In the interest of avoiding this, the lee_controller_firefly.yaml file needs to be changed. In this file the parameters for position, velocity, attitude and angular rate gain of the flight controller are set. These need to be lowered in order to avoid pivoting. The parameters used for this thesis are:

```
position_gain: {x:1, y:1, z:1}
velocity_gain: {x:1, y:1, z:1}
attitude_gain: {x:1, y:1, z:0.1}
angular_rate_gain: {x:0.4, y:0.4, z:0.1}
```

Listing 5.4: Code gains

The detailed implementation of the firefly drone won't be covered in this thesis and will be seen as a blackbox. For moving the drone towards a point, some publishers are needed, which will be covered. The goal of the potential field method is to get to the goal while avoiding obstacles. In order to accomplish that vectors are created to fly towards temporary goals, which are never reached and have only the purpose to direct the drone through the potential field towards the goal. For flying towards the temporary goals, the method go_to is created. The input parameters for this method are the desired x, y and z position and the desired quaternion for the rotation. In order to move the drone towards a point, two publishers are needed, one for a trajectory and one for the roll, pitch and yaw rate thrust. As only one point at a time will be computed, the trajectory will always only contain one point. For the trajectory publisher, a Header is needed, the name of the frame id is called 'notrelevant' because it doesn't affect the program in any way. To append one point to the trajectory, a transform object with a velocity and an acceleration needs to be created. After appending the system waits for 5 seconds in order to let the drone fly at least for a few seconds towards that direction before computing the new temporary goal. The code for the go_to method is shown in the following listing:

```
def go_to(desired_x_to_go, desired_y_to_go, desired_z_to_go, quaternion0,
    quaternion1, quaternion2, quaternion3):
    rate = rospy.Rate(1)
    firefly_command_publisher = rospy.Publisher("/firefly/command/trajectory",
        MultiDOFJointTrajectory, queue_size=10)
    another_pub = rospy.Publisher(rospy.get_namespace() +
        "/firefly/command/roll_pitch_yawrate_thrust", MultiDOFJointTrajectory,
        queue_size=10)
    traj = MultiDOFJointTrajectory()
    header = std_msgs.msg.Header()
    header.stamp = rospy.Time()
    header.frame_id = 'notrelevant'
    traj.joint_names.append('base_link')
    traj.header=header
```

```
transforms =Transform(translation=Point(desired_x_to_go, desired_y_to_go,
    desired_z_to_go), rotation=Quaternion(quaternion0, quaternion1,
    quaternion2, quaternion3))
velocities =Twist()
accelerations=Twist()
point = MultiDOFJointTrajectoryPoint([transforms], [velocities],
    [accelerations], rospy.Time(2))
traj.points.append(point)

time.sleep(15)
```

Listing 5.5: Code go_to method

With the interest of flying towards the temporary goals, they need to be computed. For this, an artificial potential field needs to be created. By using the equations 3.6, 3.8 and 3.9 the attractive and the repulsive forces can be determined. To calculate the repulsive forces by the obstacles, the obstacles need to be listed in an array. These forces can be utilized to compute a new temporary goal. The equation for calculating the new x position is:

$$x = x + rate * fx \tag{5.2}$$

Fx is the computed resulting force in the x direction and rate is a predefined variable with the value 0.5. This is needed in order to have the temporary goals in feasible distances. The equations for the y and z position are equivalent to the equation 5.2. In order to create new temporary goals during runtime, the position of the drone needs to be looked up iteratively. This is done in the move_loop method. This method has as an input the position of the view point and the actual position of the drone. The distance to the view point is calculated and while it is more than 30 cm, temporary goals are computed. 30 cm is the maximum deviation at which the view point is counted as reached. In the loop first, the new temporary goal is calculated with the help of the potential field. Afterwards, the go_to method is performed with the new temporary goal. As this method is not blocking, new temporary goals can be computed and set as new goals, while the old one is not reached, yet. To get the new actual position of the drone, a lookup between the starting point and the 'kalman' frame has to be done. In order to avoid local minima traps, the random walk method is utilized. To detect local minima traps, the last position and the new actual position are compared. If the distance between them is too small, a local minimum is found and the random walk method is performed. The random walk method is implemented a bit differently than just adding a random number to the position of the drone. By adding a random number to the position of the drone no collisions are checked. In order to not collide with obstacles, the potential field method will be utilized again. With the interest of escaping the local minima first, a random number will be created and added to the actual position of the drone. Then this new position is set as the new goal of the potential field method. With this procedure, a random walk can be created and crashes can be prevented. After checking for and escaping the local minima trap the distance to the view point is calculated again and the last position is updated, in order to avoid having an endless loop. The pseudocode for this method is shown in the following figure 5.4. In chapter 4 a method was described, if no escape from the local minima is found. The method was to direct the drone back to its starting point. As the implementation of this would go beyond the scope of this thesis, it is not realized. Instead of flying to the starting point, the drone is stopping after a certain amount of time, if no way out of the local minima is found. This method is not shown in figure 5.4 as it is part of the random walk.

```
calculate distance to view point
while distance > 30 cm:
    calculate new temporary goal with the potential field
    go_to (new temporary goal)
    lookup Transformation between starting point and 'kalman' frame
    if distance between last position and actual position < 10cm
        random walk

    calculate distance to view point
    actualise last position
```

Figure 5.4: Pseudocode move_loop

With the help of the move_loop and the go_to method, the drone can be controlled towards one view point. In order to have multiple view points, the move_loop has to be repeated for every given view point. The view points are given through a pickle file. These have to be decoded and saved in an array, called position. With the aspect of having multiple view points in the array position, a loop is needed to fly to every view point separately. With the option of flying to multiple view points, the vector flight control implementation is finished. In order to evaluate the code and proof that the concept is accomplished, some plots will be created. These will be covered in the next chapter.

CHAPTER 6

Proof of Concept

In chapter 4 a concept was presented to solve the given problem of fusing the data of two sensors and flying the drone to given view points while avoiding static obstacles. In chapter 5 an implementation of the concept was introduced. To prove that this implementation is a solution to the problem, evaluations are needed. These are separated into three sections: the Sensor Fusion Evaluation, the Vector Flight Control Evaluation and an Evaluation of the combined architecture. In the Sensor Fusion Evaluation no view points will be reached. It will be checked if the position estimated by the Kalman Filter is accurate enough and if measurement errors are balanced out. On the other hand is the Vector Flight Control Evaluation. In that section, no position estimation will take place. The position of the drone will be given from only one sensor and there won't be any measurement errors. It will be checked if the view points are reached, if collisions are avoided and if a local minimum can be escaped. Afterwards in chapter 6.3 both solutions will be combined and checked if both solutions work together so that the vector flight control is using the stabilised position of the sensor fusion. In all graphics the position will be separated in x, y and z position. Furthermore, the rotation angle, called alpha, will be shown.

6.1 Sensor Fusion Evaluation

In chapter 5 an implementation of the Kalman Filter was presented in order to match the concept, elaborated in chapter 4. If the Kalman Filter provides a solution of estimating the position of the drone and if measurement errors are outbalanced, will be checked. The evaluation of the Sensor Fusion will be separated into two parts, a non-moving part and a part, in which the drone is flying to different points. These points are predefined and mostly identical in each evaluation. The evaluation is structured in measuring the x, y and z position and the rotation angle alpha. The data given from the drone is colored blue, the data given from the simulation tool is green and the estimated position from the Kalman Filter is shown in red. The data from the drone is relative to the starting point. The data from the simulation tool is already calculated, in order to also be relative to the starting point and not to the construct. The construct origin has in the evaluations a translation from x = 2 m, y = 2 m and z = 2 m to the starting point origin. Furthermore a rotation of a quaternion with the parameters w = 0.643, x = -0.002, y = -0.727 and z = 0.242 between these coordinate frames is set. For the first tests, there are no errors from the sensors. In figure 6.1 the drone is flying to the point x = 2.0 m, y = 2.0 m and z = 2.25 m and then keeping that location. In comparison next to that figure is the figure 6.2.

In this figure, the drone is moving towards different points. In both graphics, the data from the drone and from the simulation tool is in the x, y and z position identical. This is showing, that the calculation between the different coordinate systems is successful. The rotation angle is not completely identical, due to the computation quaternion to rotation angle. As there is a maximum of 0.04 degree of deviation in figure 6.1 and in figure 6.2 a maximum of 0.12 degree of deviation, it can be neglected and can be seen as close enough to identical. The estimated position from the Sensor Fusion part, the red line, is mostly matching the position of the drone and the simulation tool. In the parts, where the drone's location has a turning point, the Kalman Filter is not completely accurate as the Kalman Filter is unable to keep up without any deviation. On the other hand, this deviation in both figures is only for a small amount of time and the estimated position is still pretty close to the actual position. Due to this, the estimated position from the Kalman Filter is accurate enough to be seen as a solution to the concept if no errors from the sensors exist.

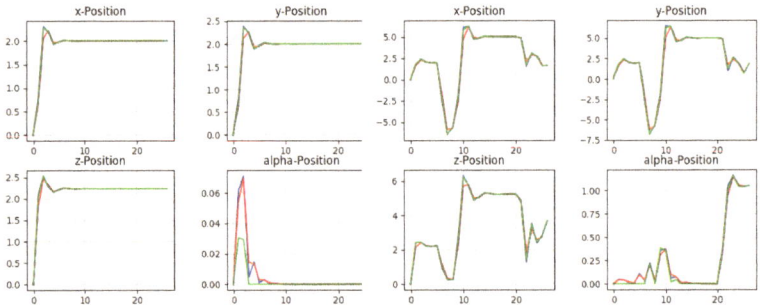

Figure 6.1: Kalman Filter without movement

Figure 6.2: Kalman Filter with movement

As errors can appear, the Kalman Filter should be able to blank them out. One mentioned error in the concept chapter is the possibility of a drift in the position given from the drone, the rotation is staying the same. The drift is increasing over time. The position of the drone should be pretty accurate despite the drift. In the figures 6.3 and 6.4 an increasing drift is added to the position of the drone. Figure 6.3 is without a movement of the drone after reaching the starting point and figure 6.4 is with a movement of the drone to multiple points. In both figures, the drift does not affect the estimated position a lot. As the drift is increasing, the deviation of the estimated position is increasing as well. The figures show that after the drift is almost 0.5m, the estimated position is starting to have a small deviation, which is less than 0.1m. As the estimated position is still pretty accurate despite the drift, the implementation of the Kalman Filter can be seen as a solution to balance out increasing drifts.

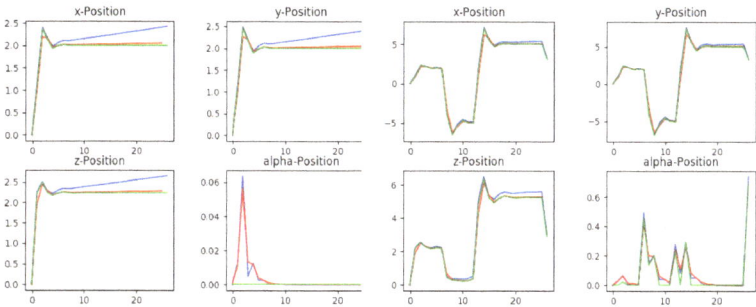

Figure 6.3: Kalman Filter without movement and drift

Figure 6.4: Kalman Filter with movement and drift

Another error, that can appear, are jumps in the simulation tool. It can happen that for a short amount of time wrong values are given. These shouldn't be considered by the Kalman Filter. These jumps are referred to the position, the rotation angle won't be affected. In the figures 6.5 and 6.6 one jump happens, which is over the value of 2. Therefore the prefilter prevents the jump to influence the position estimation. The estimated position by the Kalman Filter is not affected by this short amount of wrong values and provides despite the wrong values a precise estimation.

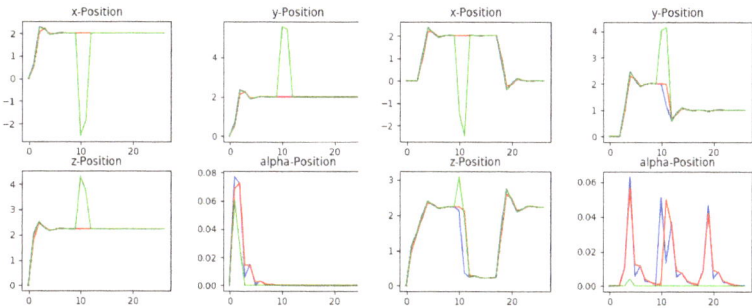

Figure 6.5: Kalman Filter without movement and jumps

Figure 6.6: Kalman Filter with movement and jumps

The last possibility of an error, that can occur, is that the simulation tool misplaces the drone in the beginning for a certain amount of time. This is simulated and evaluated in the figures 6.7 and 6.8. This error can't be balanced out as easily as the last errors. The algorithm has to decide which data is more trustful, as the data provided from the drone and from the simulation tool is not similar. In the figures 6.7 and 6.8 can be seen that the presented solution in chapter 5 is not working perfectly. In the beginning, the algorithm chooses the drone position as more trustworthy, which is correct. But as soon as the position from the drone and from the simulation are for a short amount of time equal, the algorithm decides that the position provided by the simulation tool is more accurate. In the case of the example in figure 6.7 and 6.8 the decision from the algorithm is wrong. As this error is only occurring for a certain amount of time in the beginning and the algorithm is working for a certain amount of time correctly, the outcome is acceptable. Even though there is a short period of time, in which the estimation is not accurate enough, the majority of the time the estimation is precise. Therefore the algorithm, presented in chapter 5, is still a solution for the given problem.

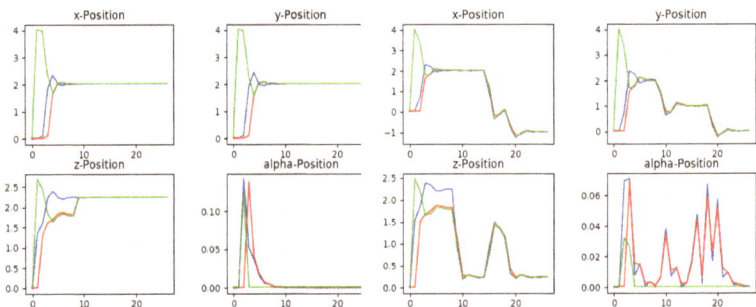

Figure 6.7: Kalman Filter without movement and beginning error

Figure 6.8: Kalman Filter with movement and beginning error

In real life, the presented errors won't only happen separately. They can be combined and for that scenario, the estimated position should still be without a large deviation to the real position of the drone. For evaluating combined errors, two scenarios are created. In the first one, the simulation tool misplaced the drone in the beginning and the position provided by the drone has an increasing drift. The second scenario has also an increasing drift but instead of a misplacement by the simulation tool, one jump is happening. In both scenarios, the rotation angle has no errors. The first scenario is presented in the figures 6.9 and 6.10, whereas the second one is shown in the figures 6.11 and 6.12. In the figures 6.9 and 6.10 can be seen, that the provided position from the drone and from the simulation tool is only for a short amount of time equal. The z position in figure 6.9 is only for one timestamp equal, which complicates the estimation of the position. After around 7 seconds the drift from the drone is noticeable and the misplacement of the drone by the simulation tool is over. Shortly before the position provided by the simulation tool corresponds with the real position of the drone, the algorithm decides to trust this position more than the position provided by the drone. Afterwards, the algorithm stays with its decision, which results in outbalancing the increasing drift. In the beginning, the algorithm is trusting the data contributed by the odometry of the drone, which leads to preventing the misplacement from the simulation inspection tool.

Even though there is a short amount of time, in which the estimated position of the drone is not completely accurate, in the long term it is getting more precise. In the beginning, the real position of the drone is resembled by the position contributed by the drone. Then there is a short amount of time, in which both given data reflect the real position, except for the z position in figure 6.9. Afterwards, the real position of the drone is mirrored in the position provided by the simulation tool. So there is a transition which data is resembling the real location of the robot. The algorithm recognised this transition, even though it is not completely the exact time as the transition happens in real-time. The deviation of the small amount of time can be neglected due to the fact that main features are recognised and in the majority of the time the location estimation is pretty accurate, which means mostly under 0.1m deviation to the real position.

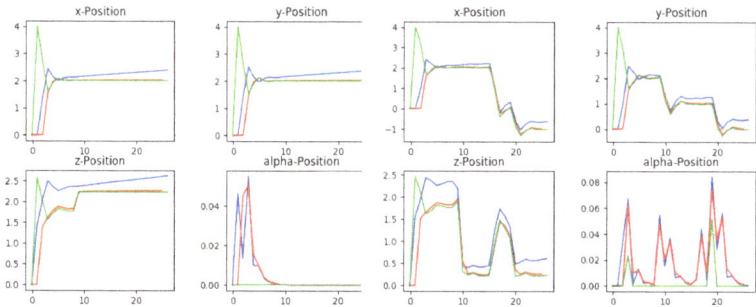

Figure 6.9: Kalman Filter without movement and combined errors 1

Figure 6.10: Kalman Filter with movement and combined errors 1

The second real life scenario is, that increasing drift and jumps can happen. In the figures 6.11 and 6.12 only one jump is happening. Before the increasing drift is noticeable, the data from the drone and from the simulation tool are similar to the real location of the robot and the estimated position is accurate. As the drift is increasing, the algorithm chooses to trust the position given by the simulation tool and bases the estimation on it. During the jump no data, which resembles the actual location of the robot, is provided. The data provided by the drone has a deviation of the amount of the drift at that time and the data given by the simulation tool is completely incorrect at that time. The position from the drone has a smaller deviation to the real position than the simulation tool. The algorithm is recognising the jump and is trusting the data contributed from the drone for the amount of the jump more than the data from the simulation tool. As soon as the jump is over, the algorithm is basing its estimation on the simulation tool data again, which resembles from that time on, the actual location of the drone. In conclusion, most of the time the algorithm chose to trust the simulation tool data, except for the time, where the data was incorrect. Therefore the algorithm based its estimation during the whole time on the data, which had the smallest deviation to the real drone position, even though it was not known to the algorithm.

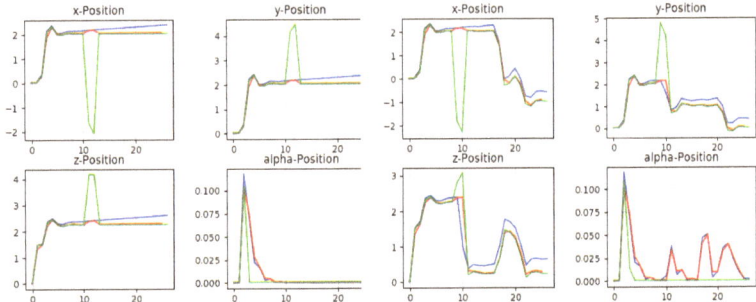

Figure 6.11: Kalman Filter without movement and combined errors 2

Figure 6.12: Kalman Filter with movement and combined errors 2

The evaluations of the Kalman Filter have shown, that errors like an increasing drift or jumps are outbalanced and don't affect the position estimation. If one of the given data is incorrect, the algorithm chooses one to give guidance to the estimation. The majority of the time the data, which resembles the real location of the drone, is chosen. In the case of a misplacement of the drone by the simulation tool, in the beginning the correct data is not always chosen. For a small amount of time, the misplaced position is as direction for the estimation selected. For all other scenarios is always the data, which has the smallest deviation to the real location of the drone, chosen. As a result, the presented algorithm in chapter 5 is a solution for the problem of estimating the position of the drone. The problem, described in chapter 1, does not only consist of the position estimation, it also consists of the vector flight control. An algorithm for solving this was explained in chapter 5. An evaluation of the algorithm will be done in the following chapter.

6.2 Vector Flight Control Evaluation

One of the main problems is to find a way for the drone to reach the given view points while avoiding static obstacles. In chapter 4 a concept was presented, which uses the potential field method to solve this problem. To utilize vector flight control in order to navigate through the potential field temporary goals are iteratively created. These temporary goals are never reached and serve the purpose of directing the drone towards the view point. For evaluating the vector flight control the position estimation from the Kalman Filter is neglected. The actual position of the drone is given by looking up the transformation between the starting point and the drone, instead of using the estimated position. In order to evaluate the solution, the goal in figure 6.13 is to reach one view point and in figure 6.14 to reach multiple view points. The given view point in 6.13 has the coordinates of x = 4 m, y = -0.5 m and z = 1 m. It is shown that after less than 30 timestamps the view point is reached. Furthermore, it can be seen that the view point is reached through steps, which are the results of the temporary goals. The ideal scenario would be, that in the graphics no steps are shown so that there is a constant movement without much deceleration and acceleration. As this goes beyond the scope of this thesis, it can be realized in future work. The rotation angle of the view point was set to 1 degree, which is also accomplished by the drone. For the multiple view point evaluation the view points $x = 4$ m, $y = 1$ m, $z = 1$ m, alpha = 1 degree, $x = 6$ m, $y = -1$ m, $z = 2$ m, alpha = 2 degree and $x = 2$ m, $y = -2$ m, $z = 3$ m, alpha = 1 degree are chosen. In figure 6.14 every view point is reached. A view point is called reached within a certain amount of deviation. In this case, the deviation is 0.3m. The figures show that the implemented algorithm is the solution for the given problem.

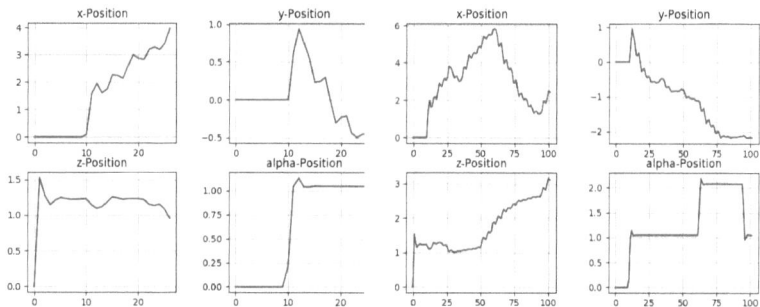

Figure 6.13: Vector Flight Control one view point

Figure 6.14: Vector Flight Control multiple view points

One problem that can occur during the potential field method, is the local minima trap. In figure 6.15 a local minima trap is shown. The view point is at $x = 5$ m, $y = -3$ m, $z = 10$ m and alpha = 1 degree. The drone is trapped around $x = 2.5$ m, $y = -0.25$ m, $z = 2.5$ m, because there are obstacles around $x = 3$ m, $y = -1$ m and $z = 3$ m. The obstacle is in the shape of the letter 'U' (shown in figure 3.4). The drone is not stopping to move, but can't escape the trap on its own. A solution presented in chapter 4 was to utilize the random walk method. This method was implemented in chapter 5. Figure 6.16 shows the movement of the drone with the same view points as in figure 6.15, but with the implemented random walk method. The random walk method created some jumps, which can be mainly seen in the x position. The random walk method was utilized three times in order to escape the local minima trap. After the use of the method, the drone could proceed with using the potential field method to reach the given view point. The view point was reached at almost the timestamp 150. Therefore it is shown, that the implementation of the random walk method is solving the local minima problem. Furthermore, in the figures 6.15 and 6.16 is shown, that collisions with obstacles are avoided. The obstacle around $x = 3$ m, $y = -1$ m, $z = 2.5$ m is never reached. In conclusion, the implemented vector flight control with temporary goals in chapter 5 is a solution for the given problem and fulfills the concept in chapter 4. The problem of reaching the view points is solved by looking up the actual position from the starting point. The concept presented in chapter 4 assumes to utilize the estimated position of the Kalman Filter as the actual position. For this, the two implementations have to be combined and evaluated as a whole system. The evaluation of the combined architecture will be covered in the next chapter.

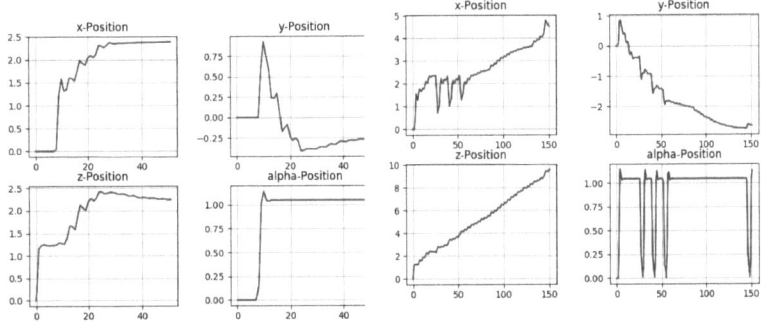

Figure 6.15: Local Minima Trap

Figure 6.16: Local Minima Trap Escape

6.3 Evaluation of the combined architecture

In section 6.1 the estimated position of the Kalman Filter was evaluated without moving to any given view points. Whereas in section 6.2 the evaluation of navigating the drone to the given view points without using the estimated position was done. In the concept in chapter 4, the proposed idea was to use the estimated position of the Kalman Filter as the actual position for the vector flight control. The implementation of the whole concept is shown in chapter 5. For evaluating the implementation of the combined architecture first, one view point is specified. In figure 6.17 the scenario is illustrated. After reaching the view point with the coordinates x = 3 m, y = 2.5 m, z = 1 m and alpha = 1 degree, the drone is flying directly to the point x = 2 m, y = 1.2 m, z = 1 m, alpha = 3 degree. It is shown that the combined architecture is able to navigate to one view point while estimating the position through the Kalman filter. In reality not only one view point is given, that is the reason why figure 6.18 was created. In that figure over 8 view points are given. All of the view points are reached by the drone and the position estimation is working without any relevant deviation. For showing that the created algorithms are solving the given problem, it has furthermore to be tested if errors in the data given from the simulation tool and from the drone affect the architecture or if the view points are despite the errors reached. In order to accomplish that two tests are created. The tests won't cover all the separate error types, mentioned in section 6.1. The first one is shown in figure 6.19. In this figure two errors are combined, one jump from the simulation tool and an increasing drift from the drone. Despite the errors, the drone is flying towards the view points and reaches them. The second evaluated error is a combined one with an increasing drift from the drone and a misplacement of the drone by the simulation tool. The evaluation is illustrated in figure 6.20. In that figure, only two view points are given, which are reached despite of the errors. The view points are x = 1.5 m, y = 0 m, z = 2 m, alpha = 1 degree and x = 2 m, y = -0.5 m, z = 2 m, alpha = 1 degree. This shows that despite errors in the given position data, the position of the drone can still be estimated pretty accurate and even though there is at some points a small deviation, the requested view points are reached.

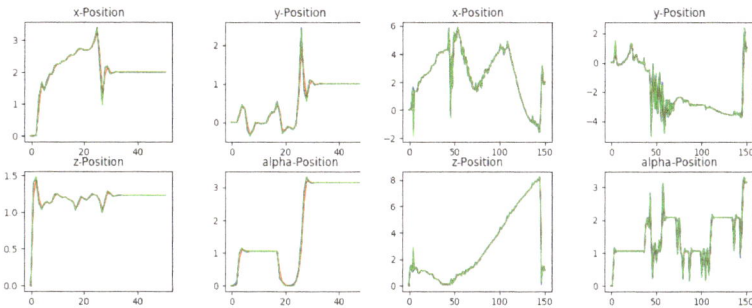

Figure 6.17: One view point   Figure 6.18: Multiple view points

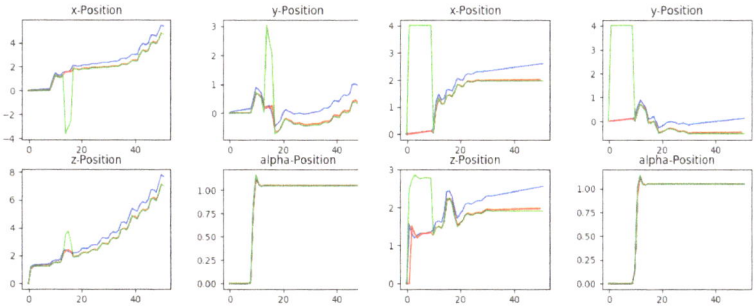

Figure 6.19: Multiple view points   Figure 6.20: Multiple view points
with errors 1   with errors 2

The conclusion is that the evaluation of the presented implementation in chapter 5 is a solution of the elaborated concept in chapter 4. In section 6.1 has been shown that through the implementation of the Kalman Filter, the position estimation of the drone is realized. This estimation can outbalance most of the errors without having a large deviation towards the real position of the drone. Even if there is a small deviation in the estimated position, the algorithm can still find a way to make the drone reach the given view points. The view points are reached through the potential field method and temporary goals. Furthermore, obstacles are avoided and the local minima trap can be escaped with the help of the random walk method. This has been demonstrated in section 6.2 and 6.3 with and without errors in the position estimation. As a summary in this chapter, it has been shown through multiple evaluations that the created algorithms provide a solution to the given problem and fulfill the elaborated concept in chapter 4. In the following chapter, a short summary and an outlook for future work will be given.

CHAPTER 7

Conclusion and Future Work

This thesis covered the project of an inspection of a large construct like a ship hull. The addressed topics of the projects were the sensor fusion and the vector flight control. The problem of the sensor fusion was to estimate the position of the drone. To estimate the position two inputs are given, the position relative to the starting point of the drone, provided by it and the position relative to the coordinate origin of the construct, provided by a software. As the software is not available, yet, it is simulated. The problem of the vector flight control was to control the drone to the given view points without colliding with any static obstacles. The elaborated concept for the sensor fusion was to first compute the position of the drone relative to the starting point from the simulation tool and then to utilize a Kalman Filter to estimate the position. In order to outbalance possible jumps, an additional filter was implemented. The evaluation of the implementation of the sensor fusion has shown that it solves the given problem. The position estimation is working within a deviation of approximately 0.1 - 0.2m, if there are no errors from the received position data. If there are errors the position estimation is still working pretty accurate, which is shown in chapter 6. Only if the drone is misplaced in the beginning by the simulation of the software, the position estimation is for a short amount of time not as accurate as desired. In future work, the algorithm could be improved to outbalance misplacements completely. The elaborated concept for the vector flight control is to use the potential field method with temporary goals to reach the view points. The temporary goals serve the purpose of directing the drone towards the view point and will never be reached by the drone. The challenge of the potential field method is, that local minimum traps can occur. For escaping these the random walk method was utilized. The implementation of the vector flight control was to calculate for each step the potential field with the given estimated position of the drone, to compute a new temporary goal within a certain step range, to check if the drone is trapped in a local minimum and then repeat the process until the drone reached the view point or multiple view points. The evaluation has shown that the implemented vector flight control is solving the given problem and furthermore, it is working while using the estimated position, provided by the sensor fusion. In the presented solution static obstacles are avoided in order to prevent collisions. In future work it can be expanded, so that dynamic obstacles, like humans, are avoided. This would be necessary if the drone is flying, while humans are working in the same room. In the evaluation of the vector flight control, it has been shown that steps occur. These appear as an effect of the temporary goals. In order to avoid most of the deceleration and acceleration, the update frequency or the distance of the temporary goals could be increased. Furthermore, the task of the future work is to transfer the work from the simulation to the real drone. For this, a software tool, which provides the position from the drone relative to the construct origin, is needed. In conclusion, this thesis provides a solution for estimating the position of the drone while outbalancing errors and a vector flight control, which directs the drone during runtime to the given view points while avoiding static obstacles and escaping local minimum traps.

List of Figures

Bibliography

[Fin+62]   David Finkelstein et al. "Foundations of quaternion quantum mechanics". In: *Journal of mathematical physics* 3.2 (1962), pp. 207–220.

[Cho92]   Jack CK Chou. "Quaternion kinematic and dynamic differential equations". In: *IEEE Transactions on robotics and automation* 8.1 (1992), pp. 53–64.

[HA+92]   Yong Koo Hwang, Narendra Ahuja, et al. "A potential field approach to path planning." In: *IEEE Transactions on Robotics and Automation* 8.1 (1992), pp. 23–32.

[WB+95]   Greg Welch, Gary Bishop, et al. "An introduction to the Kalman filter". In: (1995).

[XK97]   Xiaoping Yun and Ko-Cheng Tan. "A wall-following method for escaping local minima in potential field based motion planning". In: *1997 8th International Conference on Advanced Robotics. Proceedings. ICAR'97*. 1997, pp. 421–426.

[Sla99]   Gregory G Slabaugh. "Computing Euler angles from a rotation matrix". In: *Retrieved on August* 6.2000 (1999), pp. 39–63.

[WVDM00]   Eric A Wan and Rudolph Van Der Merwe. "The unscented Kalman filter for nonlinear estimation". In: *Proceedings of the IEEE 2000 Adaptive Systems for Signal Processing, Communications, and Control Symposium (Cat. No. 00EX373)*. Ieee. 2000, pp. 153–158.

[Ste05]   Michael Stevens. "Bayes++ Open Source Bayesian Filtering Classes". In: online, state of 29.07.2020. http://bayesclasses.sourceforge.net/Bayes++.html, 2005.

[BM08]   Luigi Biagiotti and Claudio Melchiorri. *Trajectory planning for automatic machines and robots*. Springer Science & Business Media, 2008.

[BHC08]   Y. Bouktir, M. Haddad, and T. Chettibi. "Trajectory planning for a quadrotor helicopter". In: *2008 16th Mediterranean Conference on Control and Automation*. 2008, pp. 1258–1263.

[Sha+11]   Fareed Shakhatreh et al. "The basics of robotics". In: (2011).

[CSC12]   Sachin Chitta, Ioan Sucan, and Steve Cousins. "Moveit![ros topics]". In: *IEEE Robotics & Automation Magazine* 19.1 (2012), pp. 18–19.

[EH12]   Brendan J Englot and Franz S Hover. "Sampling-based coverage path planning for inspection of complex structures". In: *Twenty-Second International Conference on Automated Planning and Scheduling*. 2012.

[Fou12]	Open Source Robotics Foundation. "XML Robot Description Format (URDF)". In: online, state of 29.07.2020. https://wiki.ros.org/urdf/XML/model, 2012.
[Mee12]	Wim Meeussen. "robot_pose_ekf". In: online, state of 29.07.2020. http://wiki.ros.org/robot_pose_ekf, 2012.
[RG12]	Julian Rothe and Dipl-Ing Nils Gageik. "Implementierung und evaluierung einer höhenregelung für einen quadrokopter". In: *bachelor thesis, Aerosp. Inf. Technol., Univ. Würzburg, Germany* (2012).
[AFG13]	Martin Riedel Antonio Franchi and Volker Grabe. "telekyb". In: online, state of 29.07.2020. https://wiki.ros.org/telekyb, 2013.
[Fou13]	Open Source Robotics Foundation. "ROS Introduction". In: online, state of 29.07.2020. https://wiki.ros.org/de/ROS/Introduction, 2013.
[Gra+13]	V. Grabe et al. "The TeleKyb framework for a modular and extendible ROS-based quadrotor control". In: *2013 European Conference on Mobile Robots*. 2013, pp. 19–25.
[Zol+13]	Yu N Zolotukhin et al. "Using the Kalman filter in the quadrotor vehicle trajectory tracking system". In: *Optoelectronics, Instrumentation and Data Processing* 49.6 (2013), pp. 536–545.
[Fou14]	Open Source Robotics Foundation. "Gazebo". In: online, state of 29.07.2020. http://gazebosim.org/, 2014.
[San+14]	Lucas Vago Santana et al. "A trajectory tracking and 3d positioning controller for the ar. drone quadrotor". In: *2014 international conference on unmanned aircraft systems (ICUAS)*. IEEE. 2014, pp. 756–767.
[Zha+14]	T. Zhang et al. "Sensor fusion for localization, mapping and navigation in an indoor environment". In: *2014 International Conference on Humanoid, Nanotechnology, Information Technology, Communication and Control, Environment and Management (HNICEM)*. 2014, pp. 1–6.
[Pet15]	B Sc Hauke Petersen. "Pfadplanung und Ausführung für einen mobilen Roboter im Kontext des RoboCup Wettbewerbs". In: Otto von Guericke Universität Magdeburg, 2015.
[Rat15]	Denise Ratasich. "Generic sensor fusion package for ROS - Source Code". In: online, state of 29.07.2020. https://github.com/tuw-cpsg/sf-pkg, 2015.
[Rat+15]	Denise Ratasich et al. "Generic sensor fusion package for ROS". In: *2015 IEEE/RSJ International Conference on Intelligent Robots and Systems (IROS)*. IEEE. 2015, pp. 286–291.
[Shi15]	Zvi Shiller. "Off-Line and On-Line Trajectory Planning". In: vol. 29. Feb. 2015, pp. 29–62. DOI: 10.1007/978-3-319-14705-5_2.

[MAV16]   Owen McAree, Jonathan M Aitken, and Sandor M Veres. "A model based design framework for safety verification of a semi-autonomous inspection drone". In: *2016 UKACC 11th International conference on control (CONTROL)*. IEEE. 2016, pp. 1–6.

[RRA16]   Victor Manuel Aboytes Reséndiz and Edgar A Rivas-Araiza. "System Identification of a Quad-rotor in X Configuration from Experimental Data." In: *Research in Computing Science* 118 (2016), pp. 77–86.

[SNS16]   Bhavin C Shah, Devendra Nagal, and Swati Sharma. "Coordinate systems for industrial robots". In: *International Journal For Technological Research In Engineering* (2016).

[Con18a]   PickNik Consulting. "MoveIt". In: online, state of 29.07.2020. https://moveit.ros.org/, 2018.

[Con18b]   PickNik Consulting. "MoveIt". In: online, state of 29.07.2020. http://docs.ros.org/melodic/api/ moveit_tutorials/, 2018.

[HO18]   Evan G Hemingway and Oliver M O'Reilly. "Perspectives on Euler angle singularities, gimbal lock, and the orthogonality of applied forces and applied moments". In: *Multibody System Dynamics* 44.1 (2018), pp. 31–56.

[Kaw+18]   Shinya Kawabata et al. "Autonomous Flight Drone with Depth Camera for Inspection Task of Infra Structure". In: *Proceedings of the International MultiConference of Engineers and Computer Scientists*. Vol. 2. 2018.

[Moo18]   Tom Moore. "robot_localization". In: http://wiki.ros.org/robot_localization, 2018.

[Sid18]   Rymsha Siddiqui. "Path Planning Using Potential Field Algorithm". In: online, state of 29.07.2020. https://medium.com/@rymshasiddiqui/path-planning-using-potential-field-algorithm-a30ad12bdb08: medium, 2018.

[Ben19]   Prof. Dr. Oliver Bendel. "Drohne". In: online, state of 29.07.2020. https://wirtschaftslexikon.gabler.de /definition/drohne-54115/version-369942, 2019.

[met19]   methylDragon. "ros-sensor-fusion-tutorial". In: online, state of 29.07.2020. https://github.com/ methylDragon/ros-sensor-fusion-tutorial/blob/master/01%20-%20ROS%20 and%20Sensor%20Fusion%20Tutorial.md3, 2019.

[Nek19]   Bc František Nekovář. "Optimal Trajectory Planning for a Quadrotor UAV for Autonomous Drone Race". In: online, state of 29.07.2020. https://support.dce.felk.cvut.cz /mediawiki/images/5/5c/Dp_2019_nekovar_frantisek.pdf, 2019.

[Lab20]   Roger. Labbe. "Kalman and Bayesian Filters in Python". In: (2020).

[Lex20]   Lexico. "US Dictionary". In: online, state of 20.06.2020. https://www.lexico.com/en/definition/trajectory: powered by Oxford, 2020.

[Ste20]   StereoLabs. "RVIZ". In: online, state of 29.07.2020.
https://www.stereolabs.com/docs/ros/rviz/, 2020.